That's My Dog!

I HAVE A POODLE

By Benjamin Proudfit

Gareth Stevens
PUBLISHING

Please visit our website, www.garethstevens.com. For a free color catalog of all our high-quality books, call toll free 1-800-542-2595 or fax 1-877-542-2596.

Library of Congress Cataloging-in-Publication Data
Names: Proudfit, Benjamin, author.
Title: I have a poodle / Benjamin Proudfit.
Description: Buffalo, New York : Gareth Stevens Publishing, 2026. | Series: That's my dog! | Includes index.
Identifiers: LCCN 2024034460 | ISBN 9781482470024 (library binding) | ISBN 9781482470017 (paperback) | ISBN 9781482470031 (ebook)
Subjects: LCSH: Poodles–Juvenile literature. | Pets–Juvenile literature.
Classification: LCC SF429.P85 P76 2026 | DDC 636.72/8–dc23/eng/20240830
LC record available at https://lccn.loc.gov/2024034460

First Edition

Published in 2026 by
Gareth Stevens Publishing
2544 Clinton Street
Buffalo, NY 14224

Editor: Kristen Nelson
Designer: Leslie Taylor

Photo credits: Cover, chrisukphoto/Shutterstock.com; p. 5 sonya etchison/Shutterstock.com; p. 7 Ruta Zukauskaite/iStockphoto.com; p. 9 (upper left) Natallia Yaumenenka/Shutterstock.com, (upper right, p. 24) topdigipro/Shutterstock.com, (lower left) Dany Store/Shutterstock.com, (lower right) Dulova Olga/Shutterstock.com; p. 11 (upper left) evrymmnt/Shutterstock.com, (upper right) OLESYA BOLTENKOVA/Shutterstock.com, (lower) OLESYA BOLTENKOVA/Shutterstock.com; p. 13, 24 (trick) sergey kolesnikov/Shutterstock.com, p. 15 Margo Harrison/Shutterstock.com; p. 17 Teemu Tretjakov/iStockphoto.com; p. 19 Nitik/Shutterstock.com; p. 21 Liderina/istockphoto.com; p. 23 sonya etchison/Shutterstock.com.

Printed in China

CPSIA compliance information: Batch #QS26GS: For further information contact Gareth Stevens, New York, New York at 1-800-542-2595.

Contents

This is my dog.
His name is Mario.
He is a poodle.

We got Mario when he was a puppy.

A puppy is a baby dog.

Poodles have curly hair.
They may look fluffy.
Hair can be
many colors.

Poodles can be
big or small.

They are smart dogs.
They can learn tricks!

Some poodles
do contests.
They jump and run!

Mario has lots of energy!

He swims well.
His webbed toes help.

Poodles like to be with their family. They like to play.

My dog is the best.
I love my poodle!

Words to Know

hair

puppy

trick

Index